15 Rules to Make Humans Act Human

15 Rules To Make Humans Act Human

Asima Bibi

Published by Asima Bibi, 2024.

15 RULES TO MAKE HUMANS ACT HUMAN

First edition. December 29, 2024.

ISBN: 979-8230779278

Written by Asima Bibi.

Table of Contents

15 Rules to Make Humans Act Human is a heartfelt exploration of the values and principles that guide us toward living a more meaningful and compassionate life. In today's fast-paced world, where materialism, competition, and self-interest often take precedence, this book seeks to remind readers of the timeless virtues that make us truly human.

Through a collection of thought-provoking stories and lessons, the book presents 15 powerful rules that serve as practical guidelines for nurturing kindness, honesty, patience, and empathy in our daily lives. Each rule is accompanied by a compelling story that illustrates its importance, showcasing relatable characters and situations that resonate with readers from all walks of life.

The stories are designed to be more than just entertainment; they are tools for reflection and growth. From tales of greed and its consequences to lessons on the transformative power of love, gratitude, and selflessness, each chapter delves into the complexities of human behavior and the choices we face. The book encourages readers to look within, challenge their assumptions, and embrace a life of integrity and compassion.

This book is not just for one type of reader—it's for everyone. Whether you are a student looking for guidance, a professional navigating the challenges of

modern life, or someone seeking inspiration for personal growth, *15 Rules to Make Humans Act Human* offers valuable insights and lessons.

By Asima Bibi

1. Table of Contents

1. Dedication

To my beloved family,

You are the foundation of my strength and the source of my inspiration. Your unwavering love, support, and encouragement have been the guiding light throughout my journey.

To my husband, whose patience and belief in me never waver, To my children, who fill my life with joy, hope, and purpose, And to my parents, who instilled in me the values I cherish today—

This book is a reflection of everything you have taught me about humanity, kindness, and perseverance.

I dedicate this work to you with all my love and gratitude.

1. Introduction

In a world increasingly driven by technology, competition, and material gain, it is easy to forget the essence of what makes us human. We often find ourselves caught in the whirlwind of daily routines, striving for success and recognition while neglecting the core values that define us as compassionate and empathetic beings. But deep down, we all crave a life of meaning, purpose, and connection—a life where humanity takes precedence over greed, pride, and selfishness.

This book, *15 Rules to Make Humans Act Human*, serves as a guiding light to rediscover and nurture the qualities that elevate us beyond mere survival. Through a collection of deeply moving stories, reflections, and life lessons, it presents a roadmap for cultivating virtues like kindness, patience, gratitude, and respect. These are not just abstract ideals—they are the foundation of a life well-lived, a life that touches the hearts of others and leaves a legacy of goodness.

Each of the 15 rules in this book is rooted in timeless principles that transcend culture, age, and circumstance. They remind us that while the world around us may change, the values that make us human remain constant. These rules are not meant to preach perfection; rather, they offer practical insights into how we can grow as individuals, strengthen our relationships, and contribute positively to society.

The stories in this book are drawn from universal experiences and reflect the struggles, triumphs, and dilemmas that define the human condition. From the dangers of greed to the power of persistence, from the beauty of love to the importance of self-awareness, these tales highlight the choices we make and the lessons we learn along the way.

At its heart, this book is an invitation to pause and reflect. In our pursuit of success and fulfillment, we often forget the simple yet profound truths that guide us toward a life of balance and harmony. Through these 15 rules, you will be reminded that:

- True wealth is found not in material possessions but in the richness of character.
- Love knows no boundaries and is one of life's greatest gifts.
- Patience and forgiveness are not signs of weakness but of immense strength.
- Honesty and integrity are the cornerstones of meaningful relationships.
- Gratitude transforms what we have into enough and fosters contentment.

15 Rules to Make Humans Act Human is more than just a book—it is a companion for anyone seeking to lead a more intentional and purposeful life. Whether you are at the beginning of your journey or looking for a fresh perspective, this book offers practical wisdom and heartfelt inspiration.

As you read through these pages, I encourage you to embrace these rules not as rigid commandments but as gentle reminders of the potential within each of us. The world is in desperate need of kindness, understanding, and humanity. By choosing to act with empathy and integrity, we can create a ripple effect of goodness that touches lives far beyond our own.

Each chapter concludes with a powerful message, distilling the essence of the story into a lesson that readers can carry with them. Whether you are seeking inspiration, moral guidance, or simply a moment of introspection, this book offers something for everyone.

Thank you for embarking on this journey with me. Together, let us strive to become the best versions of ourselves and, in doing so, inspire others to do the same. Let us rediscover what it truly means to be human.

The goal of this book is simple yet profound: to inspire readers to act with humanity in every aspect of their lives. It reminds us that true success is not measured by wealth or power but by the impact we have on others and the legacy of goodness we leave behind.

At its core, *15 Rules to Make Humans Act Human* is a celebration of the human spirit. It is a call to action for everyone to reconnect with the values that unite us and to make choices that reflect the best version of ourselves. By following these rules, we can create a world that is kinder, more just, and more fulfilling—not just for ourselves but for future generations.

This book is not merely a guide; it is a journey. A journey to rediscover our humanity and to live a life that truly matters.

Stories and Lessons

Perception

It's not always necessary to get everything you want right away; sometimes, things take time. Don't chase after every desire or make the mistake of striving for more than what's needed. Stay calm, remain patient, and maintain a positive outlook.

Stay Humble, Not Greedy

In a bustling desert town, there lived a merchant named Sameer. Renowned for his sharp business acumen, Sameer was not just wealthy—he was incredibly rich. Yet, despite all his riches, he was never satisfied. No matter how much gold he amassed, he always craved more.

One day, as the sun beat down on the busy marketplace, a mysterious traveler arrived, selling what he called the **Gem of Fortune**. "Whoever owns this gem," the traveler said with a knowing smile, "will have wealth beyond their wildest dreams. But beware—it comes with a price."

Sameer's heart raced at the mention of unlimited wealth. Without asking about the price or considering the consequences, he eagerly offered everything he owned—his shop, his house, and all his gold—in exchange for the gem. "Once I have it," he thought greedily, "I'll be the richest man alive."

At first, the gem appeared to work its magic. Sameer's luck seemed boundless. Gold coins appeared in the sand, jewels were unearthed in his fields, and priceless artifacts turned up in forgotten corners of his town. His fortune grew, and soon, he built a palace far grander than the king's. He hired servants to cater to his every whim, living a life of luxury beyond measure.

But as time passed, Sameer's insatiable desire for more began to consume him. The gem, which had once brought him so much fortune, began to warp his mind. He became paranoid, convinced that everyone around him was plotting to steal his wealth. He stopped sharing even the smallest coin, refusing to help those in need, including his closest friends.

His heart grew as cold and hard as the glittering gold he hoarded. His once joyful demeanor turned to suspicion and bitterness. Despite his vast riches, Sameer could not shake the emptiness inside him.

As the years passed, Sameer's health began to deteriorate. The gem, once a source of boundless wealth, now burned in his hands every time he touched it. His palace, filled with treasure, felt hollow, and the treasures themselves seemed meaningless. The more Sameer clung to the gem, the more it tormented him. No matter where he threw it, the gem always reappeared on his bedside table by morning.

Realizing the curse he had unwittingly brought upon himself, Sameer sought out the traveler who had sold him the gem. He found the man sitting by the edge of the town, a look of quiet understanding in his eyes.

"Please," Sameer begged, his voice filled with desperation. "Take it back! I'll give you anything—anything—to free me from this torment."

The traveler smiled gently but sadly. "The price of the gem was never your gold," he said. "It was your peace of mind. The curse you carry is not of wealth, but of greed. You will only be free when you learn that true wealth is not measured by what you possess, but by what you are willing to give."

That night, Sameer made a decision. For the first time in years, he looked beyond his own riches. He opened the doors of his grand palace to the poor, offering shelter, food, and comfort to those in need. He shared his treasures with the hungry and the sick, spreading kindness and generosity where once he had hoarded only gold.

Slowly, the curse of the gem began to lift. The burning sensation faded, and Sameer's heart softened. For the first time in years, he felt a deep sense of joy—not from what he owned, but from the happiness he had brought to others. His riches no longer weighed him down, for he had found a new kind of wealth—a wealth rooted in generosity and compassion.

Message:

Greed blinds us to what truly matters in life. True wealth is not found in what we accumulate, but in the generosity, kindness, and peace that comes from sharing with others. When we open our hearts to others, we unlock a wealth that no treasure can ever match.

Perception

Money is not everything, but it plays a crucial role in fulfilling our needs and desires. While money is undeniably important, there are certain things it cannot buy. For instance, imagine being stranded in a desert with a bag full of money but no access to water. In such a situation, money cannot quench your thirst or satisfy your hunger. Similarly, there are aspects of life that are beyond the reach of wealth. Ultimately, maintaining a balance in life is far more important than relying solely on material possessions.

Important as Money Is, It's Not Everything

In a vast desert kingdom, there lived a wealthy businessman named Omar. His reputation for riches was known far and wide, and he believed that with enough money, he could solve any problem. "With my wealth, there's nothing I cannot buy," he often boasted, convinced that money was the key to everything.

One day, Omar set out on a journey across the desert to attend an important meeting in a distant city. He loaded his caravan with luxuries: gold coins, fine silk clothes, and rare gems. However, in his pursuit of wealth and status, Omar overlooked one essential item—enough food and water for the journey.

The first few days of the trip went smoothly. As his caravan passed through small villages, he was able to purchase whatever he needed. But halfway through the desert, a fierce sandstorm suddenly swept across the horizon. The storm raged for hours, scattering his caravan and leaving Omar stranded in the vast, empty desert, with only one camel, a few bags of gold, and no provisions.

When the storm finally subsided, Omar found himself alone under the unforgiving desert sun. His throat was parched, and his body was quickly weakening from dehydration. He searched desperately for help, but there was no sign of life. The gold coins in his bag clinked mockingly with each weary step he took, their value seeming meaningless in the desolate landscape.

By the second day, Omar's strength had waned. His mouth was dry, his body frail, and his hope was all but gone. Just as he was about to collapse, he spotted a lone figure—a wandering nomad, carrying a small water pouch.

Desperate for relief, Omar stumbled toward the nomad. "Please, give me some water!" he pleaded. "I will pay you a hundred gold coins!"

The nomad looked at Omar with pity, his eyes calm but firm. "What good is your gold to me in this desert? I cannot drink it, and it will not save either of us."

Omar, nearly frantic, offered all the gold he had, but the nomad shook his head. "I only have enough water for myself," he said quietly. "If I give it to you, we'll both perish."

The realization hit Omar like a wave. He sank to the ground, staring at the gold in his hands. For the first time, he understood that money, which he had once believed could buy everything, was utterly useless in the face of survival. In the harsh desert, wealth could not quench thirst, nor could it sustain life.

By sheer luck, Omar was later found by a group of traveling merchants, who shared their water and food with him. After days of suffering, Omar was finally able to return home. But he was no longer the same man who had left his kingdom with arrogance and pride.

When he gathered his family and employees to speak, his voice was soft yet firm with wisdom. "I have spent my whole life chasing wealth, believing it was the key to happiness," he said. "But I have learned that money can buy comfort, but it cannot buy life, love, or peace. True happiness comes from balance—health, relationships, and the simple blessings of life."

From that day forward, Omar used his fortune to help others. He ensured that no one in his kingdom would suffer for lack of basic needs. He understood that wealth was not an end, but a tool—one that should be used to build a better, more meaningful life for everyone.

Message:

Money is important, but it is not the solution to every challenge life presents. There are some things—like health, love, and survival—that are priceless and cannot be bought. True fulfillment lies in finding balance and valuing what truly matters.

Perception

Everyone on Earth has an equal right to live a fulfilling and dignified life.

Never Forget: Every Life Holds Equal Worth

In a peaceful valley nestled between towering mountains, there existed a village named Harmony. It was a village unlike any other, home to people of all kinds—farmers, artists, merchants, and wanderers who had found refuge in its warm embrace. Despite their differences, the villagers lived together in peace, united by a common belief: everyone deserved a chance to live a happy, fulfilling life.

However, not everyone shared this outlook. A wealthy landowner named Malik, who owned the largest farm in the village, believed his wealth and status made him more important than the others. He often boasted, "I worked hard for everything I have. Why should I treat others the same when they haven't achieved as much as me?"

One year, a terrible drought struck the valley. The river that once flowed through the village dried up, and the crops withered under the relentless sun. Malik, who had a large reservoir of water on his land, found himself in a fortunate position. Meanwhile, many of the poorer farmers struggled to find enough water, even for drinking.

Desperate, the villagers came to Malik, pleading for water to save their families and crops. But Malik turned them away with disdain. "Why should I share my water with you?" he sneered. "I earned it through my hard work. You should have planned better, like I did."

As the drought continued, the situation became dire. People began to leave the village in search of water, but many were too weak to travel far. Malik, too, began to realize the consequences of his selfishness. Though he had plenty of water, he couldn't grow crops without the labor of the farmers he had driven away. His workers abandoned him one by one, and soon his vast farm stood empty and barren.

One evening, as Malik sat alone in his grand house, staring at the unused reservoir of water, he felt a deep sense of regret. "What use is my wealth if there's no one left to share it with?" he thought bitterly.

The next morning, something inside Malik shifted. He opened the gates to his land and invited everyone in the village to take as much water as they needed. Slowly but surely, the farmers returned, and together they worked to revive the village. People shared what little they had—food, water, and shelter—helping each other through the hardships. Their collective effort brought the village back to life until, at last, the rains returned.

Malik had learned an invaluable lesson: no matter how rich or powerful one might be, we all share this earth and depend on each other to survive. He realized that his wealth meant little without the community to support it, and that true strength lies not in material possession but in kindness and unity.

From that day forward, Malik became a humble man, treating every person in the village as his equal. His wealth, no longer a symbol of superiority, was shared freely to ensure that all could live with dignity.

Message:

Every person on Earth has an equal right to live a dignified life. Wealth, status, or power does not make anyone more deserving than another. True strength lies in kindness, sharing, and recognizing that we are all part of the same world, bound by the same needs and hopes.

Perception

To resolve a problem, you must either agree with the opposing party or persuade them to see that your perspective is correct.

Make the Decision: Yes or No, and Stick to It

In a small town nestled beside a peaceful river, two neighbors, Ayaan and Bilal, lived side by side. They had been friends since childhood, but as they grew older, their once-strong bond began to fray due to differing opinions. Ayaan was calm and logical, while Bilal was fiery and driven by emotion. Their contrasting temperaments often led to disagreements.

One summer, a dispute arose between them over a mango tree that grew on the border of their lands. The tree had stood there for many years, providing shade and sweet fruit to both families. But this season, the tree bore very few mangoes.

Bilal, looking at the sparse fruit, claimed, "The tree is on my side of the land. Whatever fruit it bears is mine."

Ayaan disagreed, saying, "The roots of the tree are on my land, and I've been nurturing it with my water and soil. I have just as much right to the fruit as you."

The argument quickly escalated, and the two former friends refused to speak to each other. Their families tried to intervene, but neither Ayaan nor Bilal was willing to compromise. The tree, silent and still, stood between them, its fruit slowly falling and rotting.

One afternoon, an elderly man named Karim, known throughout the village for his wisdom, visited the two neighbors. He had seen their quarrel from afar and decided to offer his guidance. He sat down with them and said, "You both are intelligent men, but your stubbornness has clouded your judgment. There are two ways to solve this: either you agree with each other, or you try to convince the other of your perspective. Let's attempt both approaches."

First, Karim asked, "What do you both want from the tree?"

Ayaan said, "I want to share the fruit fairly. We both benefit from the tree, and it's only right that we share what it gives."

Bilal, however, replied, "I believe the tree is on my land, and since I've taken care of it, all the fruit belongs to me."

Karim saw that reaching a mutual agreement was unlikely, so he suggested they try the second approach: convincing each other. "Now, explain your reasoning calmly, and listen to one another," he advised.

Ayaan began, "Bilal, the roots of the tree are on my side of the land. This means the tree depends on my soil and water for its survival. Without my care, it wouldn't bear any fruit."

Bilal, considering Ayaan's words, responded, "I understand that, Ayaan, but the tree stands tall on my side. Its shade falls over my land, and I've been the one to ensure it isn't cut down. Isn't that worth something?"

For a moment, they both paused, allowing the weight of each other's words to settle. Karim smiled gently and spoke, "Do you see? Both of you are right in your own way. The tree gives to both of you, just as you both have given to it. Why not share the fruit equally, just as you've shared its shade and beauty over the years?"

Ayaan and Bilal sat in silence for a moment, reflecting on Karim's wisdom. Finally, they both smiled and extended their hands in friendship. They agreed to split the fruit of the tree equally, and together, they promised to care for it so that it could continue to thrive in the years to come.

Message:

To solve a problem, you must either agree to the other person's perspective or calmly convince them of yours. However, true resolution often comes from understanding that both sides have merit and finding a middle ground. Cooperation, rather than conflict, leads to the most lasting solutions.

Perception

A man who consistently disrespects others' ideas and shows no gratitude, yet expects everyone to support and praise him, embodies selfishness and a lack of humility.

Avoid the Ego That Takes but Never Gives

In the bustling town of Ravendale, there lived a man named Simon, known far and wide for his sharp tongue and dismissive nature. Simon was tall and imposing, carrying himself with an air of superiority that made everyone around him feel small. Though he prided himself on being "practical" and "realistic," his behavior often hurt those he encountered.

Simon had one glaring flaw: he disrespected others' ideas, belittling their dreams as if they were insignificant. His neighbors learned to avoid sharing their plans with him, knowing he would either make a sarcastic remark or dismiss their ideas with a wave of his hand. At the same time, Simon demanded constant praise for his own achievements, no matter how trivial they were. He expected the world to celebrate even the smallest success he achieved, as though everything revolved around him.

One day, Simon's friend Liam approached him with an exciting new business idea. "Simon," Liam began, his eyes sparkling with enthusiasm, "I'm thinking of starting a food truck business. I've done a lot of research, and I believe it could be really successful in this area."

Simon scoffed and crossed his arms. "A food truck? Really, Liam? That's the dumbest idea I've ever heard. Who would buy food from a truck when there are restaurants everywhere? You're just wasting your time."

Liam's face fell, but Simon felt no remorse. He genuinely believed he had done Liam a favor by "saving" him from failure.

Days turned into weeks, and Simon continued his habit of dismissing others' efforts. When his neighbor Sarah shared her plan to start a charity event, Simon laughed and said, "Charity? That's a waste of energy. People should help themselves instead of depending on handouts."

However, Simon's dismissiveness didn't stop him from asking for help when he needed it. If his car broke down, he would call Liam, expecting immediate assistance. If he needed advice on finances, he would consult Sarah, demanding her expertise. Strangely, Simon always found a way to take credit for their help, spinning the narrative to make himself appear capable and resourceful.

One day, Simon found himself in trouble. His small woodworking business, which he often boasted about, began to decline. He hadn't adapted to new trends, nor had he listened to customer feedback. Desperate to save his business, he finally reached out to Liam and Sarah for ideas.

Liam hesitated but decided to offer his help. "Why not try creating custom furniture? People love unique pieces these days," he suggested.

Sarah added, "You could also promote your work through social media. I can help you set up an online page to attract more customers."

Simon nodded, pretending to listen intently. But as soon as they finished speaking, he brushed off their advice. "Custom furniture? Social media? That's too much work. I need real solutions, not pointless suggestions."

Frustrated, Liam and Sarah decided to let Simon figure things out on his own. They had grown tired of his arrogance and ungratefulness.

Months passed, and Simon's business continued to falter. One evening, as he sat alone in his workshop, he began to reflect on his actions. He thought about the people he had pushed away and the opportunities he had missed because of his unwillingness to listen. For the first time, he realized that his pride had cost him not only his success but also his relationships.

Determined to change, Simon visited Liam and Sarah the next day. "I've been selfish and unkind," he admitted. "I didn't respect your ideas, and I never appreciated your help. I want to make things right."

Though hesitant, Liam and Sarah forgave him. They knew change wouldn't come overnight, but Simon's genuine remorse was a step in the right direction. Slowly, Simon began to listen more and criticize less. He realized that respecting others' ideas didn't diminish his own worth—it enriched it.

Message:

The story of Simon reminds us that mutual respect is the foundation of strong relationships. When we dismiss others' ideas or fail to show gratitude, we isolate ourselves and lose the support of those around us. True success doesn't come from seeking constant praise but from uplifting others and embracing collaboration.

Let Simon's journey serve as a lesson: to receive kindness and respect, we must first learn to give it.

Perception

Love transcends all differences, uniting people regardless of their backgrounds or circumstances. Moreover, when you truly desire something or are deeply passionate about achieving a goal, you will find the determination and strength to overcome any obstacle to make it a reality.

When You're in Love, It Becomes the Most Important Thing in the World

Love is a curious thing—unexpected, unpredictable, and boundless. It doesn't knock at the door or send a message before arriving. It simply appears, quietly or boldly, and takes root in the most unexpected corners of our lives. There is no schedule for love, no handbook to guide us on where or how it might blossom. It simply happens, defying logic, reason, and even our own expectations.

One of the most beautiful truths about love is that it can come to anyone, at any time, in any form. It doesn't matter if you're a teenager experiencing the flutter of emotions for the first time or someone in their later years rediscovering what it means to care deeply for someone—or something. Love isn't confined to youth, nor does it fade as we age. It transcends time, space, and all societal norms, finding us when we least expect it.

And love isn't always reserved for people. Often, it stretches far beyond human relationships, manifesting itself in the connection we feel toward the natural world, animals, or even the stillness of inanimate objects. Sometimes, we fall in love with the unknown—a sense of mystery, an idea, or a dream that feels so profound it stirs something deep inside us.

Picture this: You're walking home after a long, stressful day when a stray cat crosses your path. At first, it's just another creature among many. But then it looks at you, its golden eyes shining with a quiet curiosity. Slowly, it approaches, brushing against your leg. You kneel, and the soft vibration of its purring feels like comfort in a way no words could describe. Before you know it, that cat becomes a part of your routine—a reminder of the small joys life offers when you least expect them.

Or consider the birds. Fragile yet fearless, they dart through the sky, soaring freely over the earth. Their songs fill the mornings, each note carrying the promise of a new beginning. One day, you find yourself sitting by the window, captivated by the sparrow that keeps visiting your balcony. You notice its patterns—the way it hops, the way it pecks at the crumbs you leave behind. You find yourself smiling, feeling connected to a creature that asks for nothing but gives so much joy in return.

Then there are the trees—those silent giants that have witnessed lifetimes of stories. At first glance, a tree might seem like just another part of the landscape, but spend a moment beneath its branches, and you'll see its magic. Its leaves rustle with secrets carried by the wind, its roots hold steady against storms, and its trunk bears the marks of time. You might find yourself drawn to a particular tree, sitting beneath it every afternoon, watching the sunlight filter through its canopy. Without realizing it, you've fallen in love—not with a person, but with the steadfast strength and quiet wisdom of nature itself.

Love, in its truest form, doesn't demand grandeur. It doesn't need to be shouted from rooftops or written in the stars. It's in the small moments, the gentle connections, and the quiet bonds we form with the world around us. Falling in love doesn't always mean romance; it means noticing the beauty and wonder that exists everywhere. It's the ability to pause and truly see the magic in what we might have otherwise ignored.

You can fall in love with the rhythm of the rain as it taps on your window, the scent of a flower blooming in a forgotten corner, or the way the waves crash against the shore. Love is about connection—an appreciation for the things that touch your soul, however fleeting or permanent they may be.

So, if one day you find yourself falling in love unexpectedly—whether with a person, a cat, a bird, a tree, or even a moment—embrace it. Let it fill your heart with gratitude and remind you of the infinite ways the world offers its beauty to us.

Message

Love is not limited by age, circumstance, or form. It is a gift that finds its way into our lives in unexpected ways. Sometimes, we search for it in grand gestures, but more often than not, it's waiting for us in the simplest things—a stray cat, a bird's song, or the steadfast presence of a tree.

This is your reminder to keep your heart open. Love isn't something you have to chase; it will find you when you're least expecting it, in places you never imagined. Learn to recognize it, cherish it, and let it remind you of the beauty in the world. Because love, in all its forms, is the essence of life itself.

Perception

Never imitate others, as everyone's journey and circumstances are unique. Speaking from my personal experience, I have always stayed true to myself and refrained from copying anyone. I have consistently adhered to my own principles, choosing to do what I believed was right, no matter the situation. Upholding honesty and integrity have always been my priority, relying solely on my own efforts. I firmly believe that Allah is always with me, guiding and supporting me through every step of my journey.

Be Yourself, Don't Be a Copy

In life, every individual has unique circumstances, opportunities, and challenges. These differences are what make each person's journey special and distinct. This is why copying others is never the solution to success or happiness. While it may seem easier to follow in someone else's footsteps, the reality is that their life, struggles, and experiences are not yours. By imitating others, we not only limit our potential but also lose the essence of who we truly are.

When I look back on my own life, I can confidently say that I have always chosen to walk my own path. I have never copied anyone. Whatever I believed to be right, I stood by it and acted accordingly, even if it meant being different from those around me. From childhood to adulthood, I stayed true to my principles and refused to take shortcuts, regardless of the situation.

One of the best examples of this is my experience during my school and university days. Exams, as we all know, can be a time of immense pressure. Many students feel tempted to cheat or look for ways to copy someone else's answers. But for me, that was never an option. I trusted in my preparation, my hard work, and my belief in fairness.

I clearly remember how I used to be the first to submit my exam paper. While others were still scribbling answers or looking around for hints, I would confidently hand my paper back to the examiner. This wasn't because I wanted to finish quickly—it was because I trusted my abilities and had no interest in copying others. I knew that the results I earned, whether good or bad, would reflect my own effort and knowledge.

Even outside of academics, I've always avoided copying others. Life throws many decisions our way—what career to pursue, how to solve problems, or how to live in general. I've always trusted my instincts and made choices based on my own beliefs, not on what others were doing. I've learned that what works for one person may not work for another. Our circumstances, strengths, and weaknesses are different, and what might lead someone else to success could lead me down the wrong path.

For me, the most important thing has always been faith. I firmly believe that Allah is with me, guiding me through every decision and every challenge. My faith gives me the strength to stay true to myself, even when the world around me seems to favor shortcuts or dishonesty. I know that Allah rewards sincerity, and this belief has been my constant companion throughout life.

I've also come to realize that copying others not only undermines your own abilities but also limits your growth. When you rely on someone else's path, you miss the opportunity to discover your own strengths, talents, and potential. Life is a journey of self-discovery, and staying true to yourself is the only way to truly succeed.

It's not always easy. There are moments when you might doubt yourself or feel that others are moving ahead faster because they chose an easier route. But in those moments, remind yourself of the value of honesty and integrity. Success achieved through shortcuts or imitation is never truly fulfilling. Real success comes from hard work, perseverance, and staying true to your principles.

Message:

This story is a reminder to always be yourself and trust in your unique journey. Don't waste your time trying to copy others or compare your life to theirs. Everyone has their own path, shaped by their circumstances and guided by Allah's plan.

When you stay true to yourself, you discover your own strengths, build your own success, and live a life of integrity. Remember, Allah is always with those who are honest, sincere, and hardworking. He rewards those who trust Him and rely on their own efforts rather than seeking shortcuts.

So, believe in yourself, embrace your individuality, and walk your path with confidence. Your journey is yours alone, and it's meant to be just as unique and extraordinary as you are.

Perception

Everything in this world is destined to come to an end one day, but Allah is eternal—He was, is, and will always remain everlasting. All praises belong to Him alone. Beauty, health, wealth, and even life itself are transient, subject to the inevitable changes of time. These transformations serve as profound reminders of the impermanence of worldly matters and the enduring truth of Allah's constant presence and eternal nature.

Understand that all things, good or bad, come to an end.

In a small village nestled at the foot of a mountain, there lived a wise old man named Yusuf. He had lived many years, seen countless seasons come and go, and witnessed the changes in the world around him. People from all over the village sought his advice, whether it was about love, family, or the challenges of life. Yusuf's wisdom was respected, but it wasn't his words alone that made him so revered—it was the calm way in which he lived, accepting the ebb and flow of life's changes.

One day, a young man named Amir, who had just lost his job, came to visit Yusuf. He was troubled, feeling as though everything he had worked for had come crashing down around him. His health was declining, his relationships were strained, and his financial stability seemed to be slipping away. Desperate for guidance, he approached Yusuf, hoping for some sort of answer that could restore the balance he had lost.

Yusuf welcomed him into his humble home and invited him to sit. "Tell me, my son," Yusuf said, "what troubles you?"

Amir poured out his heart, speaking of his failed career, his crumbling health, and the uncertainty of his future. "I have worked so hard for everything I have," he said, "but it feels like it's all slipping away. I'm afraid that I'll never regain what I've lost."

Yusuf nodded thoughtfully and led Amir to the garden behind his house. It was full of blooming flowers, trees, and shrubs, but Yusuf stopped in front of a rose bush that was beginning to wilt. "Do you see this rose?" he asked. Amir nodded, observing the fading petals. "It was once beautiful, full of life and color. But now, it is changing, as all things do."

Amir looked puzzled, unsure of where the conversation was leading. Yusuf continued, "The rose didn't resist the change, and neither should you. Everything in this world—whether it is wealth, beauty, or health—is subject to change. Life is full of seasons—some are bright and full of growth, while others are dark and challenging. But none of them last forever."

Amir thought for a moment and asked, "So, should I simply accept my losses?"

Yusuf smiled gently. "It's not about simply accepting defeat. It's about understanding that change is natural. Your job, your health, your wealth—they are all temporary. They are blessings, yes, but they are not permanent. The only thing that remains constant is the presence of Allah. His wisdom, His mercy, and His eternal nature are what we should rely on."

As Amir listened, he began to understand what Yusuf meant. He had been clinging to the things he had lost, unwilling to accept the inevitable changes that had come into his life. But now, he realized that resisting change only brought pain. Yusuf's words opened his eyes to the impermanence of the world, and he began to see his struggles not as failures, but as opportunities for growth.

Yusuf continued, "The rose will eventually bloom again, just as you will find new opportunities in your life. Trust in the process, trust in yourself, and most importantly, trust in Allah's plan for you."

Amir felt a sense of peace wash over him. He had spent so much time focusing on what he had lost that he had forgotten to see the potential for renewal. He thanked Yusuf and promised to embrace the changes in his life, knowing that every season had its purpose, and that everything, good or bad, was part of a bigger plan.

Message:

Life is full of change, and it can be difficult to accept the things we lose along the way. But remember, everything in this world is temporary—beauty, health, wealth, and even life itself. What remains constant is the eternal presence of Allah, who guides us through every trial and every season of our lives. Embrace change with faith, trust in Allah's wisdom, and know that every challenge is an opportunity for growth. Allah's plan is greater than any loss, and His eternal love is the one thing we can always count on.

Perception

Always strive to control your anger, as words spoken in the heat of the moment can leave lasting consequences and cannot be taken back.

Your Strongest Weapon Is Patience

In a small town by the river, there lived a man named Tariq, known for his quick temper. Though he was successful in business and well-respected in the community, he struggled to keep his emotions in check, especially when faced with frustration. His family and friends often found themselves walking on eggshells, unsure of when Tariq's temper might flare.

One afternoon, Tariq had an argument with his business partner, Zayd. It started as a minor disagreement—about the allocation of resources for a new project. However, as the discussion progressed, Tariq's frustration grew. His voice became louder, and his words more pointed. Zayd, a calm and collected man, tried to reason with Tariq, but it was no use. In the heat of the moment, Tariq snapped, shouting harsh words that he would later regret.

The argument ended with Tariq storming out of the office, leaving Zayd sitting quietly, his face expressionless. Later that evening, as Tariq sat at home, the anger began to subside. He replayed the argument in his mind, realizing that he had crossed a line. The words he had said in anger were harsh and unnecessary, and he knew they had hurt Zayd. Tariq felt a deep sense of regret. He realized that he had let his emotions control him, and now, the damage had been done.

The next morning, Tariq woke up feeling uneasy. He couldn't focus on his work, as the guilt gnawed at him. He knew he had to make things right, but he wasn't sure how. After much thought, he decided to visit Zayd and apologize. When he arrived at Zayd's office, he found him sitting calmly at his desk, working. Tariq took a deep breath and walked in.

"Zayd, I owe you an apology," Tariq began, his voice sincere. "I lost my temper yesterday, and I said things I shouldn't have. I didn't mean them, and I deeply regret how I acted. Please forgive me."

Zayd looked up from his work and smiled gently. "Tariq, we all make mistakes. What matters is that you recognize it and are willing to make amends. I accept your apology."

Tariq felt a weight lift from his chest. He had taken the first step toward making things right, and Zayd's calm response reassured him that forgiveness was possible. As they sat down to discuss the project again, this time with mutual respect and understanding, Tariq couldn't help but feel grateful for Zayd's patience.

Over the following months, Tariq worked hard to control his temper. He began practicing mindfulness and took time each day to reflect on his emotions. He also sought guidance from a trusted elder, known for his calm demeanor and wise counsel.

One day, while reflecting on his progress, Tariq realized how much his life had changed. His relationships were stronger, and his business was thriving. He had learned that patience and self-control were powerful tools that could prevent unnecessary conflict and protect the harmony in his life. More importantly, he had learned that his anger, when unchecked, could not only harm his relationships but also tarnish his reputation.

Message:

Anger is a natural emotion, but when allowed to control us, it can lead to regret and damaged relationships. It's important to remember that once words are spoken in anger, they cannot be taken back. Learning to control our temper and respond with patience can transform our interactions and preserve the peace in our lives. Reflecting on our actions and seeking forgiveness when necessary allows us to grow and build stronger, more respectful relationships. Always strive to control your anger, for in that control lies the power to nurture understanding, harmony, and trust.

Perception

People tend to value you based on their own level of understanding, rather than recognizing your true worth.

Stay away from those who undervalue you.

In a bustling city lived a man named Ibrahim, who had always prided himself on his work ethic and kindness. He was a skilled craftsman, known for creating beautiful wooden furniture that people admired. His work was sought after by both the wealthy and the modest, but despite his talent and dedication, Ibrahim often found himself feeling unappreciated.

His shop was nestled in a quiet alley, away from the main streets, where most of the wealthy people passed by. The rich preferred to shop in the grand stores on the city's busiest avenues, believing that expensive, mass-produced furniture would bring them the quality they desired. Ibrahim's hand-carved pieces, though filled with soul and attention to detail, were often overlooked by those who could afford them.

One day, a wealthy merchant named Omar walked into Ibrahim's shop. He had heard of Ibrahim's work but had never been interested in visiting. His taste in furniture was heavily influenced by trends and status, and he assumed that high prices were the true measure of quality. As Omar entered the shop, he took a quick glance at the simple yet elegant wooden chairs and tables, dismissing them with a sneer.

"I hear your work is highly praised," Omar said condescendingly, "but I've never understood why people would pay so much for something so... ordinary."

Ibrahim looked at Omar, calm and composed. "Sir, my work may not be adorned with gold or silver, but it is crafted with care and passion. Each piece tells a story, and it is made to last a lifetime, not just to impress in a moment."

Omar chuckled. "But no one will care about the story of your furniture if it doesn't have a reputation. People only value what they see in the grandest shops, what is advertised as expensive and rare."

Ibrahim remained quiet, not arguing, but simply watching the merchant as he continued to examine the furniture with a critical eye. After a while, Omar turned to leave, his mind already set on his next shopping destination. "I believe I'll find better elsewhere. Your work is good, but not for someone of my status," he said dismissively as he walked out of the shop.

Weeks passed, and Ibrahim continued to create his furniture with the same dedication. One day, a young couple, Miriam and Ali, entered Ibrahim's shop. They had heard of his craftsmanship from a friend and were eager to see his work. As soon as they walked in, they were captivated by the beauty of the wooden pieces.

Miriam walked up to a beautifully carved chair. "This is exactly what we need for our new home," she said, her eyes bright with admiration. Ali nodded in agreement, smiling at Ibrahim. "It's not just the craftsmanship that draws us in, but the love and effort that went into creating this piece. It feels like it was made just for us."

Ibrahim smiled warmly, his heart full. He could feel that Miriam and Ali truly appreciated the value of his work—not just the physical beauty, but the time, effort, and passion that went into it. They did not look for the grandest or most expensive pieces. They saw the true worth in what was handmade, sincere, and meaningful.

As Miriam and Ali left, Ibrahim felt a sense of satisfaction that went beyond money. He realized that people often value what they understand or what reflects their own level of thinking. Omar, driven by his need for status, had judged Ibrahim's work by its price tag and outward appearance, while Miriam and Ali, who valued sincerity and craftsmanship, saw the true value in his hands and heart.

Message:

People tend to value others based on their own level of understanding, often overlooking what truly matters. It is important to remember that true worth is not always reflected by outward appearances or societal standards. What matters most is the passion, dedication, and authenticity we put into our work and our lives. The right people will always recognize your true value, even if others fail to see it. Keep believing in yourself, and let your worth be defined by what you create, not by how others perceive you.I will suggest Stay away from those who undervalue you.

Perception

The most difficult task of all is convincing people of the truth, for truth is not fabricated and often challenges preconceived notions.

Though it's tough, truth always wins in the end. (The greatest challenge of this century is believing in the truth, as it is unfabricated).

In a small village surrounded by lush green fields, there lived a young man named Amir. He was known for his wisdom beyond his years and his unwavering commitment to the truth. Unlike others in the village, Amir did not concern himself with what was popular or accepted by society. He sought only the truth, even when it was difficult or unpopular.

One day, a rumor began circulating in the village. The village elder, a man respected by all, was accused of dishonesty. People whispered that he had taken money from the village's charity fund and used it for personal gain. The accusation spread quickly, and soon, everyone in the village was talking about it. The elder's reputation, which had taken years to build, was suddenly in jeopardy.

Amir, who had always respected the elder and admired his wisdom, was troubled by the rumor. He had spent many years learning from the elder and knew him to be a man of integrity. However, the whispers of the villagers were growing louder, and many began to believe the accusations without question.

As the days passed, Amir's internal struggle grew. He knew that the elder was innocent, but he also understood the difficulty of convincing others of the truth. People often believed what was easiest to accept, especially when the truth was uncomfortable or difficult to prove. Amir knew that if he spoke out, he would face opposition and could risk alienating himself from the village.

One afternoon, Amir gathered his courage and went to see the elder. The elder, sitting alone in his modest home, looked up as Amir entered. "Amir, my child, what brings you here?" he asked, his voice calm and steady.

"I've heard the rumors, Elder," Amir said, his voice tinged with concern. "I know they are false, but no one seems to believe me. People are so quick to accept what they hear without seeking the truth. How can I convince them that you are innocent?"

The elder smiled softly, his eyes filled with understanding. "The truth is often the hardest thing to defend, Amir. People are quick to believe what they hear because it is easier than questioning what they have always known. But the truth is not something we can fabricate. It stands on its own, even if it is not immediately accepted."

Amir sat silently for a moment, pondering the elder's words. "But how do we stand against the lies when they spread so easily?" he asked.

"You must speak the truth, Amir, even when it feels like no one will listen," the elder replied. "The truth does not need to be fabricated, for it will always be revealed in time. Your job is to remain steadfast, to share it with conviction, and to trust that it will eventually find its way to those who are willing to listen."

Amir left the elder's home with a renewed sense of purpose. He knew that speaking out would not be easy, but he also knew it was the right thing to do. The next day, he stood before the villagers in the town square. His heart raced as he addressed the crowd that had gathered, eager to hear what he had to say.

"My friends," Amir began, his voice steady but full of emotion, "I stand before you not to argue, but to share the truth. The rumors you have heard about our elder are false. I know him, and I know the kind of man he is. He has never taken from this village for himself, and he has always acted with honor. I urge you to question the source of these rumors and to seek the truth, for it is not what is easy to believe, but what is right."

The crowd murmured in response, many still unsure whether to believe Amir's words. But some listened, and in time, they began to see the truth for themselves. The elder's reputation was slowly restored, not because of flashy arguments or fabricated proof, but because of Amir's unwavering belief in the truth.

Message:

The most difficult task is convincing others of the truth, especially when lies are easier to believe or more widely accepted. The truth is not something we can fabricate to fit the narrative of others; it stands on its own. When faced with adversity, we must remain steadfast in our commitment to truth, even when it is unpopular. Over time, those who are willing to listen will recognize it. Stay patient, speak with conviction, and trust that the truth will always prevail.

Perception

Truth cannot be hidden; one day it will always come to light.

Truth cannot stay buried; it will eventually come to light.

In a small village nestled between mountains, there was a man named Haris who was known for his honesty and integrity. He worked as a carpenter, crafting beautiful furniture for the villagers. His reputation was spotless, and he was trusted by all who knew him. However, beneath his calm exterior, Haris carried a secret that he had hidden for years.

Years ago, Haris had made a mistake—one that he was ashamed of. He had been involved in an incident where a valuable piece of wood, which had been entrusted to him for crafting, had been stolen. Haris had been in a difficult situation at the time, financially struggling to support his family. In a moment of desperation, he had taken the wood for himself, believing he could replace it later. But when he realized the consequences of his actions, Haris became consumed by guilt. He hid the truth, hoping that no one would ever discover what he had done.

As time passed, Haris worked hard to rebuild his reputation. He became known as one of the most skilled carpenters in the village, and the villagers trusted him completely. Yet, no matter how successful his business became, the weight of his secret never lifted. Every time he crafted a beautiful piece of furniture, the guilt gnawed at him. Deep down, Haris knew that his secret could not remain hidden forever.

One day, a stranger arrived in the village, a merchant who had traveled from a faraway land. He had heard of Haris's skill and came to purchase a few of his finest pieces. The merchant was a man of keen observation, and as soon as he saw Haris's work, he immediately noticed something strange. A particular pattern on one of the tables looked oddly familiar to him. He had seen the same pattern in his own homeland, on a piece of furniture made from a rare type of wood.

Intrigued, the merchant asked Haris where the wood for the table had come from. Haris hesitated, a cold sweat forming on his brow. He knew that the truth was about to catch up with him. He tried to dismiss the merchant's question, but the man was persistent.

"Please, tell me where you found this wood," the merchant insisted, his voice calm but firm. "I recognize the pattern—it's from a rare forest that only a few have access to."

Haris's heart raced as he realized that the merchant knew more than he had expected. There was no escaping the truth now. With a heavy heart, Haris finally confessed. He told the merchant about the stolen wood and the guilt that had haunted him for so long.

To Haris's surprise, the merchant did not react with anger or judgment. Instead, he nodded thoughtfully. "I knew the truth would come to light one day," the merchant said. "But what matters now is how you face it. You have carried this burden for so long, and now you must find a way to make amends."

The merchant's words struck Haris deeply. He had spent years hiding the truth, afraid of the consequences, but he now realized that the only way to truly heal was to confront his past.

With the merchant's encouragement, Haris went to the village elder and confessed everything. He admitted his mistake and asked for forgiveness.

The elder listened carefully, and after a long pause, he spoke. "The truth cannot be hidden forever, Haris. But by coming forward, you have shown great courage. Your actions from this day forward will determine how you are remembered, not the mistakes of your past."

Haris felt a weight lift from his shoulders. Though he still had to work to rebuild the trust he had lost, he knew that by facing the truth, he had taken the first step toward redemption. The villagers, moved by his honesty, forgave him and supported him as he made amends.

Message:

The truth cannot be hidden forever. No matter how carefully we try to conceal our actions or our past, eventually, the truth will come to light. It may be uncomfortable, and it may be difficult, but it is always better to face the truth than to live with the burden of secrets. In acknowledging the truth, we not only free ourselves but also open the path for healing and redemption. Remember, it is not the mistakes we make that define us, but how we choose to learn from them and grow.

Perception

You tend not to value something precious and rare if it comes to you too easily. However, it is important to reflect on yourself and show respect and appreciation for what you have or what you've received.

Never overlook something precious, even if it comes easily—always appreciate it

In a quiet town nestled by the sea, there lived a young woman named Sarah. She was known for her beauty and charm, but what few people knew was that she often took the good things in her life for granted. Sarah came from a well-off family, and everything she desired—whether material possessions or relationships—seemed to come effortlessly. Her parents provided her with everything she needed, and people around her always offered help without her asking. To Sarah, these things were just a part of life, things she expected to receive without much thought.

One summer day, as Sarah wandered through the town's marketplace, she overheard a conversation between two elderly women. One of them spoke of a rare necklace she had once owned, a gift passed down through generations, made with precious stones that shone like the stars. The other woman sighed, "It's a shame it was lost in the fire. That necklace was a treasure."

Sarah's curiosity piqued. She approached the women, asking, "What was so special about this necklace?"

The first woman smiled warmly at Sarah. "It wasn't just the beauty of the necklace, dear. It was the meaning behind it. It was given to my grandmother when she was married. It symbolized love, family, and the bond that tied us all together. It wasn't something you could buy at a store or acquire easily. It was earned, passed down with pride, and it held memories that no amount of money could replace."

Sarah listened intently, but a part of her didn't fully understand. She had always been accustomed to getting things easily, whether it was compliments or material possessions. To her, the necklace seemed just like any other piece of jewelry—something nice but not extraordinary.

As weeks went by, Sarah's thoughts kept drifting back to the necklace. She began to reflect on the things she had been given in her own life—the love of her parents, the friendships she took for granted, and the comforts she enjoyed without giving them a second thought. She began to realize that she had never truly appreciated what she had because it had always come easily to her.

One day, while taking a walk along the shore, Sarah stumbled upon an old fisherman mending his net. He was an elderly man, weathered by the sun and salt of the sea. His face was lined with years of hard work, and his hands were rough from decades of labor. Sarah struck up a conversation with him, curious about his life.

The fisherman smiled at her and shared his story. He had spent his entire life working on the sea, battling storms, and toiling every day to provide for his family. He spoke with pride about the simple things he had—a small house, a few crops in his garden, and the love of his children. "I may not have much in the way of riches," he said, "but the things I hold dear are priceless. They weren't given to me easily. I had to work for them."

His words resonated deeply with Sarah. She had always taken everything she had for granted, never fully understanding the value of what she possessed. The fisherman's humble words made her realize that the most precious things in life were often earned through hard work, sacrifice, and appreciation—not simply handed to you.

In the weeks that followed, Sarah began to change. She started to look at her life with new eyes. She took time to appreciate the love and support of her family and friends, no longer assuming it would always be there without effort. She also began to give back, helping others in small ways, whether through volunteering or simply offering a kind word. Sarah understood now that the things that truly mattered were not the things that came easily, but the ones that were earned through time, effort, and gratitude.

Message:

It's easy to take things for granted when they come too easily. We often don't realize the value of something precious until it's no longer in our possession or we've had to work hard for it. True appreciation comes when we reflect on what we have, the effort it took to get there, and the importance of showing gratitude for the things that matter most in life. Whether it's love, friendship, or opportunities, never forget to appreciate the things you have before they slip away.

Perception

For example, a person trying to launch a small business or pursue a passion despite facing constant failures may encounter financial challenges, personal doubts, and external criticism. However, through persistence and resilience, their efforts gradually yield results. This demonstrates the valuable lesson that progress is often slow, but consistent and steady efforts ultimately lead to success.

Keep your eyes on success, not the hurdles.

In a bustling city filled with opportunities, there lived a young woman named Laila. Ever since she was a child, she had dreamed of starting her own bakery. She loved to bake—cookies, cakes, pastries—and she poured her heart into every batch she made. Her friends and family always praised her treats, telling her she had a special gift. But Laila knew that starting a business was never as simple as it seemed. There were countless obstacles awaiting anyone brave enough to pursue their dreams.

When Laila turned 26, she finally decided to take the leap. She had saved up just enough money to rent a small shop space and buy basic equipment. With excitement and determination, she set up her bakery, calling it "Sweet Dreams Bakery." Her heart swelled with pride as she prepared her first batch of cookies, envisioning customers lining up to buy her creations.

But the reality of running a business was far harder than Laila had imagined. Despite her talent in baking, the bakery struggled to attract customers. The foot traffic was low, and many of the people who passed by seemed uninterested. Laila worked tirelessly, trying to market her bakery through social media, offering discounts, and even handing out free samples. However, after months of hard work, her sales remained dismal.

As the weeks turned into months, Laila faced constant setbacks. She couldn't afford to hire staff, so she spent long hours baking and managing the store alone. Her financial situation became more desperate with each passing day. The rent was due, and there was barely enough money for ingredients. There were times when she wanted to give up, to close the shop and forget about her dream. The weight of failure began to feel unbearable.

To make matters worse, Laila faced external criticism. Friends and acquaintances who once encouraged her now questioned her decision to start a business. "Maybe you should have chosen a safer path," some would say. "Baking isn't a steady income, Laila. You're just throwing your money away." The doubts crept in, and Laila found herself questioning whether she was cut out for this after all.

One particularly difficult evening, after yet another day of slow sales, Laila sat alone in her bakery, feeling defeated. She stared at the empty counters and the shelves filled with unsold goods. "Why am I doing this?" she whispered to herself. "Maybe they were right. Maybe this was all a mistake."

Just then, the bell above the door jingled, signaling a customer entering. Laila looked up to see an older woman with a warm smile, holding a basket. The woman walked up to the counter and said, "I've heard so much about your bakery. I wanted to try your cookies."

Laila hesitated but then smiled, offering the woman a plate of freshly baked cookies. "These are my best batch," she said quietly.

The woman tasted one and closed her eyes with delight. "These are amazing," she said. "I've been to bakeries all over the city, but nothing compares to this."

"Thank you," Laila replied, her heart lifting just a little.

The woman paused for a moment before speaking again. "You know, the best businesses are built on persistence. You're good at what you do. It might take time, but you're on the right path. Don't give up now."

The words resonated with Laila deeply. She had heard similar encouragement before, but this time it felt different. It wasn't just a fleeting compliment—it was a reminder that success wasn't about overnight achievements. It was about consistency, hard work, and the willingness to keep going when everything seemed impossible.

The following weeks weren't easy. Laila still faced many challenges, but her perspective had changed. She didn't focus on the immediate failures anymore. Instead, she concentrated on making small improvements every day—perfecting her recipes, experimenting with new flavors, and finding creative ways to reach more customers. Slowly but surely, her efforts began to pay off. Word of mouth spread, and more people started coming into Sweet Dreams Bakery. Her social media following grew, and with it, her sales.

By the end of the year, Laila had turned her business around. Her bakery was no longer struggling to stay afloat; it was thriving. She had learned that success wasn't about instant results. It was about persistence in the face of adversity and the courage to continue when the road ahead seemed uncertain.

Message:

The journey to success is never without obstacles. There will be moments of doubt, failure, and criticism. But true progress comes from persistence. It is not the instant successes that shape us, but the steady efforts we make, day after day, despite setbacks. If you believe in what you're doing, keep going. Your hard work will eventually pay off, and one day, the success you've worked so hard for will be within reach.

Perception

A broken heart can never find peace, even when it is buried beneath the soil. Therefore, never try to break someone else's heart.

Never Take Someone's Heart for Granted

In the small town of Willowbrook, there was a young man named Adam, known for his charm, good looks, and his easygoing nature. He had the kind of presence that made people gravitate toward him, and for a long time, he reveled in the attention and admiration he received. Adam was never one to commit to anything long-term—whether it was relationships, jobs, or promises. He believed that life was about enjoying the moment and moving on without being weighed down by anything.

There was a girl named Lily, a quiet and thoughtful soul who worked at the local bookstore. She had been watching Adam from a distance for months. Though she noticed his carefree attitude, she saw something deeper in him—a vulnerability that no one else seemed to notice. They had shared a few conversations over the counter at the bookstore, and Lily found herself drawn to his charisma, despite the warnings from her friends.

One day, Adam walked into the bookstore, and without any preamble, he approached Lily. "Hey, would you like to grab coffee sometime?" he asked with his signature smile. Lily's heart fluttered, and she nodded, not wanting to seem too eager but unable to hide the excitement that bubbled within her. They set a date for the following weekend.

Over the next few weeks, Adam and Lily spent more time together. They laughed, shared stories, and even talked about their dreams and fears. For Lily, it felt like everything she had hoped for. She admired his free-spirited attitude and the way he seemed to embrace life without hesitation. She thought that maybe, just maybe, this was the start of something meaningful.

But as the days passed, Adam's behavior began to change. He started canceling plans, becoming distant, and not replying to her texts as quickly as he once had. Lily felt the shift, but she told herself it was just a phase. Perhaps he was busy with work or personal matters. But deep down, she couldn't ignore the growing unease in her heart.

One evening, as they sat together at a café, Adam looked at Lily and said, "I don't think we're really right for each other." His words hit her like a sharp blow, the kind that left her breathless and numb. She blinked, trying to process what he was saying. "What do you mean?" she asked, her voice trembling.

"I like you, but I think I'm not ready for anything serious. I don't want to lead you on," he explained, looking anywhere but at her.

Lily felt her heart shatter in that moment. It wasn't just the end of a relationship she had hoped for; it was the realization that someone she had trusted had broken her heart so carelessly. She didn't know what to say, so she just nodded and left the café quietly, her mind swirling with a storm of confusion and pain.

In the following days, Lily couldn't shake the hurt. She tried to carry on with her life, focusing on work and spending time with friends, but the ache in her chest lingered. She couldn't stop thinking about Adam, wondering why he had made her feel so special just to turn away when things became real. What was it that made him pull away when she had opened her heart to him?

Weeks later, Adam crossed paths with Lily again, but this time, it was different. He looked at her with a sense of regret in his eyes. "Lily," he began, "I just want to say... I'm sorry. I didn't realize how much I had hurt you."

Lily looked at him, and for a moment, she could feel the weight of his apology. But the pain of the past lingered. "You hurt me, Adam," she said softly. "But what hurts even more is knowing that you never really cared. You didn't give me a chance to show you who I really am. You just walked away without a second thought."

Adam was silent for a moment. "I was afraid of what a real relationship would mean. I never wanted to hurt you. I just... didn't know how to handle it."

Lily took a deep breath, the pain of his words still sharp but slowly fading. "I understand, but just remember—broken hearts never truly heal, even when buried deep. You can't just walk away from someone's heart and expect them to forget."

With that, she walked away, feeling a sense of closure, she hadn't known she needed. It wasn't easy, and she wasn't completely healed, but she had learned that love isn't something to be taken lightly. It's a gift that deserves respect, and once it's broken, it leaves scars that time alone may not fully heal.

Message

A broken heart can never find peace, even when buried beneath the soil. It's easy to hurt others without realizing the impact of your actions. Treat others with kindness, respect, and honesty, for the wounds you create can last a lifetime. When you love, love truly—and never take someone's heart for granted.

Some Insights

About the Author

About the Author:

Asima Bibi is an author and a seasoned professional with over 11 years of experience in plant-related work. Her interest in storytelling spans genres, and she has written extensively about various subjects, from traditional medicine to thrilling mysteries. Asima's work often explores complex characters and hidden truths, offering readers an immersive experience. She is based in Abu Dhabi, UAE, where she enjoys blending her personal and professional experiences into her literary works.

www.ingramcontent.com/pod-product-compliance
Lightning Source LLC
LaVergne TN
LVHW040956150826
845672LV00002B/726